2.20.20	4
Headlines	7
Hey, How You Making Out?	10
A Bit More, A Bit Less	13
If I Could Make Rain Fall	15
Family Memoirs: 2013	16
Gilligan's Island	18
New Hobby: Watching Short Films	21
Flying Spirit	22
Pay The Light Bill	23
FaceTime	25
Black Ties:	27
A History of Black Ties	27
An Occasion of Black Ties	28
A Black Tie Affair	30
The Island of Misfit Toys	32
Advertisement Interlude: The Binge Pill, Coping For Dummies	35
The God of Destruction	41
She Recalls Her First Horror Movie	42
The Start of An All Encompassing Journal	43
My First Official Journal Entry: June 21th 2020	46
Burn The Rose	46
Finding You...	47
This Pen Doesn't Work	48

Doctor. Doctor?	50
A Father's Parable To The Cloud..	53
A Mother's Parable: Mind of A Butterfly	56
Crisis Actor	59
Personal Observation: I Talk A Lot	60
Journal Entry: Feelings	61
Forever	61
In Here	61
The Worst Pain	62
This Is My Perspective On What Covid Relief Meant To Me, Feel Free To Fuck All The Way Off	63
Human Nature	65
Just Be A Building	66
Journal Entry: July 12th	68
Marathon	70
Journal Entry: August 2nd	72
A Brighter Blue	72
Public Confession: What I Have To Say	74
Journal Entry: Documenting a Summer of Protests	75
Uncle Sam	75
Carson Oliver Patrick-Simpleton	78
Journal Entry: November Reign	82
November 2008	83
November 2016	85
American President: A Comparative Essay Sparked By A FaceTime Conversation About	

	3
the Last Eight Years	88
Understand	94
Watching Short Films: This One Is About Friends	97
Libations	99
2.21.21	101
Discontinued	103
Appendix: Notes & Acknowledgements	106
Special Acknowledgments	110

2.20.20

I thought today was going
to be a beautiful day.

The air was rustic
The frenetic breeze
whimsically blew through
the recuperating leaves of the trees.

As the current brushed to, through & past
The sun caressed the grass
like a ballerina does at a recital:
Delicately gliding to, through & past
the stage caressed by grace.

I woke up joyous;
Like happily & together-
Joy us-
No joy is what I experienced
with open eyes to the sunlight
and glorious striding tides
latching onto a beach that
holds on tight to the sunset.

I thought today was going
to be a beautiful day.

And then it just wasn't.

The air once rustic
forever turned rusted
as it begun to become
rested in my lungs.

The frenetic breeze
chilled ever so callously
causing me to wheeze
as air swooped & swapped
with blood in my nasal pass.

As the current brushed to, through & past
I thought about it all.
The good times & the troubled ones.
Instantly the current became too current.
Flickering through memories together
they just stop abruptly
mimicking damaged vcr tapes.

Honestly no matter how scenic
or pleasant today was to become
it was always destined to be nothing
worthy of praise.
Because quite frankly today

we became aware that we will have
to lay you in your final resting place.

Headlines

Shareef Colingsworth was found dead in Tulsa, Oklahoma earlier today.

One headline read,
"White assailant in a police uniform allegedly shoots and murders another promising young black male in Tulsa, Oklahoma: a city with a rich history of discrimination and racial injustice".

The article mentioned
the tragic story of Black Wallstreet
the tumultuous story of 60's and 70's
race relations in the city and how
the terrifying reality of racially motivated crimes persists today as another
black man is on the receiving end.

People took to Twitter to share their anger, their frustration, their outrage
and the newest hashtag
#JusticeForShareef✊✊✊

Shareef Colingsworth was brought to Lourdes Hospital where he was pronounced dead at

5:47pm as a result of complications brought on
by the three bullet wounds that pierced his heart,
lung and liver.

Another headline read,
"In Tulsa, Oklahoma the Tulsa police quickly took
action to protect nearby shoppers as a distressed
lady proclaimed to have seen a thug wearing a
black hoodie with a gun,"

The article mentioned
the rise violent crime and how
city streets in America are
being ravaged with Covid & Homicide.
The writer advocated for law and order
and a no tolerance policy on rioting
to bring the country out of chaos.

I didn't read the articles.
I couldn't focus on the words;
They were just there.
Reading me as I scrolled past
More and more lost after every sentence.

First shock.
Then confusion.
More shock.

Next dissociation.
Finally nothing.

Blank.

B l a n k.

Blank.

New Headline.
Really the only line that is now repeating in my head over and over and over again.
"My best friend is gone".

Hey, How You Making Out?

9:53am 2/21/20
Veronica: How you making out?

10:32am
Me: typing...
Me: With my tongue● lol I'm good wassup?

Veronica: Lollll you got issues● I wanna go out & grab lunch● Are you free?

Me: I wish I could but I got work●

Veronica: On a Saturday●

Me: Yeah, I gotta finish this QBR report. Sorry maybe next time, we'll figure something out.

....

2:47pm 2/23/20
Trista: How you making out?

2:55pm
Me: typing...

Me: Like a pornstar⬤ lol I'm good wassup?

Trista: Lmao ⬤ Me, Abdul & Derek wanted to go see Birds of Prey at the AMC tomorrow. Are you busy? You should come with us!

Me: I would love too but I already made plans to chill with Angel⬤

Trista: ⬤⬤We can reschedule it if you want. We really want you to come, it won't be as fun without you⬤

Me: that's fine, I appreciate it but it's cool. Y'all can go on with me. We'll find something else to do soon💯 Talk later, I'm bout to go get something to eat.

....

8:31pm 2/27/20

Derek: Ayo wassup, haven't seen you in a minute and wanted to check in with you. How's everything?

9:42pm

Me: typing...
Me: As good as it ever was and could ever be 💧💯

Derek: Aight, just wanted to make sure because everybody's been tryna chill with you and you've been more M.I.A than paper planes.

Me: Lol nah, I've just been busy with work and had car issues and shit. It's all good though.

Derek: Aight because I heard about what happened to Shareef and I'm sorry● If you need to talk you know I got you✊

Me: typing...
Me: typing...
Me: stops typing...
Me: starts deleting...

Message deleted.

Me: Aight my guy, thanks. I'll let you know if I need to talk about anything. I gotta go but I'll hit you up💯

A Bit More, A Bit Less

As a preface I know this conversation
is going to be a difficult one so let me start off
by saying I think what we have is good.
Buuuuuuttttttttt it's not perfect.
Don't get me wrong, I want to get it to be-
just as you want to get it to be-
and for it to be perfect
we don't have to put much of any work in,
Just a little more and less here and there.

Like I was thinking we should
do some more self discovery
and find out more about ourselves...by ourselves.

I still want to take you to beautiful places...
Just not with me to every place every time.

Like I was thinking we need to occupy
more time in each other's' minds
and spend a bit less time by each other's sides.

I still want to take you out on dates....
Just on less dates on the calendar.

Like I was thinking we should stay close
and to take it further I think it might
be good to be a bit more closed off as well.

Now I hear you.
We should get back into the habit
of saying good morning and goodnight
a bit more...while everything in between
can be shared a bit less.

I really don't know how to put it-
I think what we have is good
But I'm not feeling too great-
I'm not feeling too great about it.

If I Could Make Rain Fall

If I could make rain fall
I would flood every inch
of asphalt & concrete
my family, friends and friends
that I consider family
travel on.

If I could make rain fall
I would flood every inch
of thought & dream
my family, friends and friends
that I consider family
rest upon.

If I could make rain fall
I would flood every inch
of skin on my cheek &
my family, friends and friends
that I consider family
would notice how I feel,
temporarily halt their days,
and provide the love & support
that I desperately need.

Family Memoirs: 2013

Do you still have that
old beat up photograph
of Uncle Louis from a while ago?

I'd like to see the coffee stain
covering his motorcycle,
feel the cut corner at the bottom left
next to your little scooter,
and place my hand on the
silky smooth fabric while
remembering the crisp Autumn air
of that day back in 2013.

Do you remember that day Taylor?
He taught you how to ride
a bike without the training wheels.
Under his word you mastered it-
riding so fast you nearly rode it
till the wheels were about to come off.

I remember that day very well,
I keep on replaying it hoping it would
help me to learn what he taught you.

Can I see the photograph Taylor?
I need to remember what it was like
before our worlds' lost their training wheels
and spiraled out of our control.
I'm falling off as I'm failing to get a grip on reality.
My hands no longer on the handle bars,
I have no sense of control and
I don't know where this road leads.

Gilligan's Island

Island.
No passenger ships
Just solo cruisers.
No intimacy
No Intermingling
No vulnerability
Population I
Parameter me.

Island.
Just food for thought
Raindrop on the brain.
Sand in your hand
Slipping out the
Cracks in your hand
Back down the drain.

Island.
I am landing-
I landed-
No I still fall down
I don't get up-
I'm not getting up-
Can't get myself up

Till the day is nearly up.

Island.
Remote vacation
Channel surfing
Unearthing series-
Lack of urgency
To keep up with things
To keep up with
Day to day needs.

Island.
Lost like Gilligan.
No map, no key to be free
Feeling trapped again.
Feelings trapped again.

Island
Disheartened.
I am
Hardened.
I drift drift drift away
From Pangea-
The sea disconnects us
Don't know if I'll ever see her.

Island.

Palm trees
Beach
Sunny skies-
Clear skies-
This isn't a reflection of me
This doesn't represent my life.

Island I am
Stormy weather
Typhoon-
Spiraling loose
Against the lagoon
Crash-
Island I am
Not together
Crass-
Lacking tact
Impact slacking
Steady missing in action-
Enacting no passionfruit
Island I am
Bird, with a feather, no flock
No group, just wasting my youth.

Island.
No man is an island
But this is I land.

New Hobby: Watching Short Films

I watch short films now.
Have you ever heard of the
YouTube channel Omeleto?

Well they got tons of them.
Attention grabbing-
Adventure themed-
Absurdly compelling ones too.

I've been watching the channel
over the past week to pass the time by
and keep my mind occupied.

I set time to watch them with friends too.
Collectively interacting-
Together assembling-
Sharing experiences.

I watch short films now.
They're one way we can stay connected
despite having to stay separated.

Flying Spirit

There are people who can travel freely,
leaving everything behind them.

I'm a person that brings the places
they've been to everywhere they go,
Carrying luggage that no one person
should have to claim.

But the extra baggage
is nothing more than a carry on,
And carry on is exactly what I intend to do.

Pay The Light Bill

As an adult you are responsible
for your own light bill.
Do yourself a favor and pay it.

Pay it everyday,
Pay it however you may,
Pay it because there will be
Storms & storm clouds that will relentlessly
attack & attach to your place-
Pay it because if the lights
ain't on they won't be gone.

It's hard to keep the lights on.
They didn't teach me this
in high school or college
but this knowledge is
absolutely positively
vital for your survival.

Sometimes you will barely be scraping by.
60 hour work weeks
Working six days a week
Weary and wrestling fatigue:
I know your situation will get hard but

You still have to keep your lights on at all times.
You cannot afford to let them
get turned off even as you sleep.

If you like to work out, go to the gym.
If you love to read, then buy a good book and read.
If you need to watch tv to keep your peace
watch some short films.
Do what you need to do to keep the lights on.
Life is too short for you to stay in a dark place.

FaceTime

FaceTime.
The world misses you.
Mask mandates &
personally prioritizing space
have helped make it hard
to feel close to those who we relate.

I rue rejecting offers to go out
with my friends while we still could.

FaceTime.
The world needs to.
Universal unrest &
globally grieving chests are burdened
with regret as they can't see loved
ones before they are laid to rest.

I rue rejecting the opportunity to see
my uncle while I still could.

FaceTime.
The world still has you.
Contagious complexions &
sillily smiling affections

can still be shared from a screen
to another screen and to another
person who we share connection.

I dislike reimagining how to socialize
but I relish knowing that it's still possible
to connect with those I care for most in my life.

Black Ties:
A History of Black Ties

Dressed for the reoccurring occasion,
She stands upright in the humid heat.

Full figured & legs branched out,
She stands as the outright star in the pasture.

Weighed down against her will
She stands with a tie accessorized by
a faded jewel.

Partly covered now with drenched roots,
She stands berated as pests catcall
and ravage her matured jewels.

The year is 1836, she is 30 her jewel 26.
The year is 1866, she is 60 her jewel 17.
The year is 1901, she is 95 her jewel 22.
The year is 1965, she is 159 her jewel 19.
The year is 2020, she is 214 her jewel 21.

The year is the future,
She is an aging Bur Oak tree,
Her jewel is another young black man.

Black Ties:
An Occasion of Black Ties

Rebelliously red, the charred ribs
come out perfectly grilled from the pits of hell.
Triple melt oven-baked Mac N Cheese,
Greens, beans, potatoes (salad), tomatoes-
all that and a bag of chips!
My mouth has tasted the glory Hallelujah!
This here sanctified food is nourishment
for our bodies and bless'ed be
the hands that made it!

Singing on one accord but many
different disheveled chords
we are lead by the sacred scripture
"You don't know nothing bout this".
Belting imperfect harmonies along
to revered hymns by our dearly beloved
Whitney, Bobby, and archangel Micheal
to name a few.

The newest attendees teach
praise dance routines on the grass
that surrounds the temple steps.

The amused church folk scream and shout from
their pulpits disguised as lawn chairs.

Little brothers and step-sisters,
Cousins and grandmothers,
Cousins-in-law and godfathers,
friends & friends we consider family,
Aunties and Uncle all unified
under the heavenly summertime daylight.

All are in attendance for this
sanctimonious & transcendent
occasion of black ties.

Black Ties:
A Black Tie Affair

There's reasons why we wear
black suits and ties to these events.

Solid black suit, striped black tie.
This outfit symbolizes the hardships
we've endured.

Solid black suit, polka-dotted black tie.
This outfit symbolizes the destinations
we've traveled to.

Solid black suit, solid black tie.
This outfit symbolizes the future
we didn't make it to.

There's reasons why I'm wearing
a black suit and solid black tie.

It's basic.
It's boring.
It's bland.
It's this pastor and his eulogy-
It's this elaborate ceremony-

and it's going to be more of the same
in an hour at the cemetery.

Soon you'll fill the grave that was dug out in remembrance,
For years to come I'll feel the void formed in your absence.

The Island of Misfit Toys

I'm Broken
I just no talk no more.

I have an arm-
Actually I got two of 'em.
But something is wrong-
Something is always wrong.
I'm tall and I'm long
but I got no reach-
Oh how I long to reach out
to someone but I got a broken arm.
Actually,
I got two of 'em.

I'm broken.
I just no work no more.

I have a leg-
Actually I got two of 'em.
But something is wrong-
Something is always wrong.
I can walk and stride
but I tried to stand and I can't-
I can't hold myself up-

I wanna carry the load I picked up
myself but I got a broken leg.
Actually,
I got two of 'em.

I'm broken.
I just no dream no more.

I have an eye-
Actually I got two of 'em.
But something is wrong-
Something is always wrong.
I can look and stare
but everywhere is blank-
I desperately want to envision the better future
that my broken eyes are too flawed
to capture and translate back to me.

I'm broken
I can't feel anymore.

I have a heart,
Actually the remains of a heart.
For some time it's been gone-
For a while it's been gone.
It used to jump and beat
but now it skips beats

mostly a flat line
it ain't as upbeat as it used to be.

I'm broken.
I can't play anymore.

I'm worse off than a basketball with a hole,
I'm worse off than a hungry hippo with parts missing,
I'm worse off than a chess board without either king;
The brokest toys like me have everything,
everything that needs to be fixed
but may not be able to be fixed.
I'm just not good enough as is-
As is, I'm just another misfit.

Advertisement Interlude: The Binge Pill, Coping For Dummies

Hello, Are you currently
struggling to make ends meet?
Got too many bills like a McDermott huddle?

Do you have too many thoughts
circulating to fall asleep?
Twisting and turning in your bed because
the same thoughts keep entering your head?

Are you just not ready to take on even
life's simplest responsibilities?
And above all else you feel like you need
something to cope with everything?

Well you're in luck!
Introducing the not-at-all revolutionary
and totally counterproductive
Binge Pill!

With just one pill a day
you'll be able to avoid all life's troubles
while recklessly satisfying yourself with
life's incredibly underwhelming indulgences.

Not sold yet?
Just listen to some stories from
some of our top abusers!

"Hey, ish ya girl Monique an' I been
Taking the binge pill for almost a year now.
Lemme tell you how I've been catching
up on all my shows.
Desperate Housewives,
Mobwives,
Real Housewives-
Forgetting How To Be A Housewife-
Alladat and then some!
Girl I've watched entire series in days
An' I can pull an all-nighter of movies
with No Trouble.
My man left me because
I stopped paying him attention
And started paying for Hulu, Netflix and
YouTube Red subscriptions but it's okay.
I mean it's not and my heart is broken
But I don't need tissues cause this is still better
than the drama of dealing with all these issues,"

Don't have cable?
No problem,
We can still connect you

with anything you choose to misuse!

"Hi, my name is Bill and I have been
taking the binge pill for 3 months now
and, don't get me wrong,
life is still shitty but it doesn't
bother me anymore.
When I take the binge pill,
I binge eat everything to
overcome my incessant sadness.
I eat pancakes, bacon and eggs with
my leftover steak, potatoes and
mac and cheese for days and still
I can't get enough-
I don't take A lunch, break at work-
No I take 3 of em'!
My boss has damn near had it with me-
And so has my wife and chil'ren.
I'm eating us out of house and started
nibbling on the home while
she cooks and bakes dinner and dessert alone.
I even eat when I'm asleep-
It's horrible but gloryful compared to confronting
my issues constructively,"

What's that?
Food isn't your thing?

Well don't you worry
we got other options
that will still get the job done in a hurry!

"Hey I'm Ted.
I was worn out before
I found out 'bout these here Binge Pills.
I was always working and stressing and
wondering 'bout everythang-
I ain't like myself back then.
The beauty is I don't know if I like myself
now but I don't think 'bout it no more.
I've been on these for 'bout two years
now I guess.
I sleep from sunrise to that 'der sunset.
I've been sleeping like a baby-
The type of baby that cries when they
Awake and throws 'dem temper tantrums.
I never know what day it is-
Actually everyday is Sunday
Because the good lord told me
to rest and that's what I do.
I got too darn tired of working myself to death-
I got up one day and thought
"Hell, I might as well sleep myself into debt,"
And true as the sky is blue that's what I did.
The sky is still blue...right?"

Still a little skeptical.
Sleep doesn't do the job either for ya huh?
Take my advice, we got a pill for every vice!

"Hello, it's Marie
And the pill has just changed my life
in so many ways since it came out
I can't explain!
For one I'm a casual drinker,
I drink so casually all day everyday.
I even offered the officer a sip
when he pulled me over-
I thought it was a nice gesture,
but he didn't take that lightly.
He searched me and found a lighter,
cocaine and traces of some PCP.
Court was brutal, rehab was harder
but hardest was the time spent
dealing with my problems.
I got back to binge drinking and drug use
as soon as I was approved to go home.
I don't plan to ever stop taking the Binge Pill.
Even at its worst it's still heavenly in comparison
to dealing with what I've been going through
indefinitely.

Find out for yourselves
Why 0 out of 10
therapists and counseling
practitioners recommend
The Binge Pill!

Do-not-take-if-you-are-pregnant-may-become-pregnant-have-heart-problems-liver-disease-high-blood-pressure-want-to-maintain-a-healthy-lifestyle-want-to-have-a-healthy-lifestyle-want-to-cope-with-trauma-in-a-healthy-way-want-to-cope-and-not-avoid-your-issues-in-an-unhealthy-manner-care-about-your-future-breathe-air-or-need-air-to-survive

The God of Destruction

I just wanna reach out into the sky
and strangle the sun and watch as
all the glorious light it's been holding
onto for so so long pours out
onto the middle of nowhere.

I just wanna harness it's heat so I can burn
past the beautiful layers of skin, wool & fur
of the living and watch their souls
melt in my callous hands.

I just wanna gain its mass
so my thoughts weigh in as I yell them at the
tip of my lungs trying to give insight into the
black hole that is forming out of my essence.

I wish I could sit down and watch
as the flowers die roses and blue,
I wish I could look down and watch
as even the insects suffocate violetly red.

I want to bend down and observe life crumble
because I want to destroy in the same way that
destruction has become me.

She Recalls Her First Horror Movie

It was a gory scene.
Blood dripped ominously,
skin serrated & scattered,
tapping time onto the tiles.

It was a suspenseful scene.
Tears dripped slowly,
bare bones berated
showcasing an inebriated waltz in the pool.

It was an urgent scene.
I fearful, frightened & frenzied
Searched for a phone,
Searched for a pulse,
Searched for hope.

The scene was revelatory.
Thoughts flowed continuously,
while waiting & ruminating
in the emergency room
I continued to search.
Search for a reason why
and a solution that we could find.

The Start of An All Encompassing Journal

Last week I had what I'll call a small episode and my girlfriend, Elle, was there and witnessed the aftermath.

Anyway a couple days later I come home from the liquor store and I see Veronica, Trista, & Derek on the living room tv. Elle used my PlayStation USB port to hook up to her MacBook and did a group FaceTime. I thought it was some type of socially distanced intervention. Thinking to myself "what the fuck is going on?". I was confused and I thought of my uncle taking us, me & my cousins, which are his kids, or were his kids (shit), to the state festival where we had the most amazing fried cotton candy ever—

Anyway they said they all noticed a change in me since Shareef's death. They mentioned how I had been canceling plans and bailing out on them even before the shutdown. They went on about how I've been to myself & isolated for months now and some other shit that I zoned out on. I was wondering about Shareef's girlfriend, Ariana, and how she was holding up. I hadn't seen her since I was at Shareef's mom's house about a week ago to check on her——

Anyway, they suggested I see a counselor. They gave me a list of counselors they had vetted that worked with my insurance and at that point I couldn't say no. So I met with Kimberly yesterday. She's nice and listens to me-not sure what the hell she thinks of me but I guess I'll find out soon enough. She suggested that I keep a journal of my thoughts before I go to sleep so that's what I'm doing today. I never know what to say but she says that I should just write my thoughts as they come. She also said that she would like to go over my journal with me-whatever I was comfortable enough to share with her-so but I don't know if there's anything worth saying that I haven't already. I mean I do talk a lot——

Anyway, I'm no stranger to writing, just haven't done so in a while so I'll take the opportunity to get back to doing something I'm used to and vaguely I'm used to. Last week I was in a crazy place but I think things are a bit better. Kinda scared of "counseling"-I mean I'm not crazy. But I guess I like talking to someone. I'm just gonna keep journaling & writing because I think it's fun—

Anyway I think ima just take a binge pill and go to sleep now. I'll journal tomorrow or whatever. Guess it's not talk soon since this is all me writing to myself, maybe I'll say "write back soon"…whatever we'll figure it out. Or I will. Something like that.—

Anyway, till another time.

Today's Date: June 18th 2020

My First Official Journal Entry: June 21th 2020

I wasn't so sure if I could even find any words to say yesterday so I just skipped it entirely. This whole journaling thing is much more difficult to get used to than it seemed at first. I wrote a couple things earlier about how I feel and I was hoping I could use it as a jumping off point and start there. I copied them down below:

Burn The Rose

Imagine
the pedals
of a pink rose
perpetually
burning away
in a wildfire
leaving only a
charred stem behind,

One day that stem
will grow to represent
how I feel today.

Finding You...

You were there
   For one moment,
One moment in
   Time...

I turned around

And when I looked back,

You were gone.

                Why did you leave me?

                      And where did you go
        That was so much better than being

Here
With me

This Pen Doesn't Work

Never had this penman
witnessed such a broken pen.
Journey with me to the land
of snow-coned Cap
short for Captivity
at an angle, unfavorable
with a jarring, jar lid
no wonder crooked lettering
skid, letting strangers in
enter this is now a slim stalk-
failed retainer, waster of lushest
black chalk, big talk and declarations of
finished papers decor-
Like décor?
Like you agree that this
cylinder is, a still ender
leaving wonders about
what good could still be in there
in'a, inner layered dysfunction—
no I'm lying this wasn't
a poorly crafted pen
but a fine tool of invention
given, power of dimensions
4th wall break ins

shakin', foundation
so why doesn't this utensil
do what it used to do anymore?

It must be something missing in the ink.

Doctor. Doctor?

I abused pain pills and now
my friend's have prescribed me a visit.

The doc asked me who I was
and how I got to be this way-
I don't like questions or even
when I'm questioned,
I don't know why—
And so it was with my response.

She asked me about family,
I have none...
or no answers that is.
I don't know why I don't
feel loved like I should.
I don't know why I don't
avoid arguments with the
knowledge that I could-
I don't know why I don't trust
people even though I should-
and I don't want to accept why what happened
had to have happened
even though I know if I were
in the right state of mind I would.

She asked me what I do to cope.
I said I self medicate,
I love to drink
I love to smoke
I hate to hope
I even moved from fantasizing about
cutting my wrist to considering
slashing my throat-
She asked why can't I stop.

I told her her that
from my experience no doesn't mean no
and that stop really means go,
For example...
go texting and driving,
go speeding
and go running through red lights-
She said my case was severe;
I could've told her that...
and actually I did.
Anyway she scheduled me
an additional appointment
for emotional therapy.

At first it didn't really sit right with me.
Why because I've been going and

I've been trying but I feel like she's been lying
She said it would help but the only thing
that could is the needle on the shelf-
the bottles of alcohol I start and finish myself-
and the cocaine I sniff till my nose melts.

I get high partially because
I'm not fit for the ground.
And it works better than
talking my issues over a 1-800 pound
So doctor doctor just let me be.
I'm not entirely sure about counseling
but this deep feeling sure has got a hold on me.

A Father's Parable To The Cloud..

darkened by the grief of beauty
you keep holding on
and on to every last drop.

tender and grey
the sunlight is beaming down across your back
but not implanting its happiness into your soul,
it's making you visibly
weak and softening your insides
into a pool of nothingness.

you're so big
and yet so gentle.

you're so friendly
but yet so
Alone.

you're a sensitive soul that hasn't
been felt the right way.
that's why you just float around
being led by the wind.

while in that quiet time

where you pretend to flaunt and perform
as if the rays of life
have swam beyond your surface,
I watch you take shape in secret.

water pours out
from your pockets
releasing the lumped and clumped up
acids, toxins and even traces of pollution.

and when it pours
oh my does it pour.
pounds upon pounds
come down drenching
the earth beneath you.

as you roam
from one end to another end
you wonder if you're wrong for the way you are.
you're not wrong the way you are,
you are not even the only cloud
in the sky that is the way you are.

to the cloud that this pertains to
continue to be you
continue to float.
past these stormy mountains

lies your own sunny coast.

A Mother's Parable: Mind of A Butterfly

Your sophistication is mummified;
learn to live to let go.

I remember when you were younger;
before you became naive.
You were a skilled visionary
taking your thoughts and making
them into something I could only dream.

Did you let the weight of the world cover your
shoulders as you grew older?
Did it take you from your life in the clouds
and place you on these harsh grounds?

I found you in your web searching
in the leaves for a way to leave.
Are you searching for a way to leave-
you can tell me, I won't judge.
I ask because I'm concerned.

I can hardly recognize you-
are these just for show or do you really
want to drag around this furry coat everywhere
you go?

You aren't this slime you leave behind.
It might be your past but It just isn't you.
Remember, you are always more than what
happens to you so no matter what happened
to you it will never become you.

But I've seen that you've made it apart of you;
I couldn't help but notice your striped
and colored coat of thick skin.
Why did you try to harden yourself
with a cocoon of silk?
We both know that your soul is soft cotton;
you feel everything.
You can pretend but I know the coarse earth
will still scrape against your belly
even if you say you can handle the mantle.

So why continue to move forward?
I think by now you've figured out that
you weren't meant to walk.
Is that why you've chosen to crawl?
Well I have news for you,
you weren't meant to do that either-
you were meant to fly and nothing less.

Unwrap your headscarf and let your wings

do what they were meant to;
I know you think your cocoon is protection
but really It's just held you down since its
inception.

It's not too late to change,
don't let what happened
stop you from achieving your dreams.

Crisis Actor

The sky fell.

Like Henry Caville
I walked outside ready to catch clouds.

Like Michelangelo di Lodovico
I arranged the pieces into a mosaic.

Like Jeffry Hudson
I played the role of a fool.

The sky fell.

And yet I thought putting on a brave face
was enough to restore it to its right place.

Personal Observation: I Talk A Lot

I enjoy talking.

Usually about philosophy
but unusually about history,
mathematics, clouds, butterflies
my Forrest Gump spiel
and everything in between.

I enjoy talking
but I don't say anything.

For years I've talked people to death,
and only recently have I realized that
what I don't talk about will lead me to my own.

Journal Entry: Feelings

I know I have to be honest and open about how I feel if I want to grow and get through this. It's challenging being this vulnerable but anything is possible with persistence. I tried writing about my feelings a few times the past couple of days and each time I think I was able to dive a bit deeper. Here's what I wrote:

Forever

The shortest word
I have ever come to know.

In Here

It's so beautiful out.
It makes me wonder though,
If words like warm, nice, and surreal
can describe what it's like out there,
then why can't those same words
describe how it feels in here?

The Worst Pain

The worst pain I have ever felt can be likened to a
serrated knife engraving hieroglyphics directly
to your heart for weeks without pause;
Something you can't translate but
you understand deeply enough to crush your
soul.

The online newspaper article gave
me a razor sharp paper cut;
weakening & providing an opening
for an opportunistic virus to continue to ravage
me.

I've lost and I've broken bones
but nothing compares to the pain
that the loss of loved ones will bring.

This Is My Perspective On What Covid Relief Meant To Me, Feel Free To Fuck All The Way Off

I would like to give a big congratulations
to the government of the United States
& it's citizens for the excellent job
done during this pandemic.

In the United States
Covid Relief didn't mean
monthly checks to supplement income
like in most of Western Europe.

In the United States
Covid Relief didn't mean
a two week total shutdown
to halt the spread of the virus
so we could return to normal
like Australia and the Pacific coast.

In the United States however
Covid Relief did mean
politicizing science and safety measures
like wearing masks.

It meant pleading every day to
fellow citizens to not congregate
in large groups and go out to parties in vain.

Needless to say in the United States
Covid Relief meant that hundreds upon
thousands of people had to die
unnecessarily because of the selfish actions
of politicians, conspiracy theorists,
& otherwise normal people.

Above all else in my own life,
Covid Relief meant early retirement as
my only uncle is no longer with us:
Forever relieved from having to be alive
to bare witness to the bullshit that's lodged
in the toilet and holding human existence
up from societal progress.

Bravo,
A captivating and worthy display put on
by the greatest country on earth.

Human Nature

If you're reading this
from the other side
of the ongoing apocalypse
and want to study
us humans and our nature
All you need to know is this:

We were able to develop guns,
helicopters, and nuclear weapons
used to massacre one another
but we may never cure cancer,
solve homelessness, or learn
the concept of compassion.

Just Be A Building

It's a mentality.
A perspective-
A point of view that can only
be understood by a few.

Not understood by the few as in
the few, the proud the marines-
the few as in the feud:
the rare ones whose only experience
at a beach is the storm at Normandy.

Like I said, It's a mentality.
A perspective-
A point of view that can only
be understood by a warrior.

Not understood by the warriors as in
what's your warrior,
the warriors as in those who have
gone through and not forgotten
the bombshell debris that once
covered their feet.

For as long as I can remember

I've always been a rare one.
But fuck it.

From this day forward,
I choose to be a building.

It's a declaration.
An objective-
A mission statement that may
fly over the heads of those
that haven't lived the life
that I've gone through.

My street may be covered with violent graffiti-
my apartment may not be fully furnished-
my faucets may be leaky-
but believe me as long as I stay building
my current situation will not define me.

Journal Entry: July 12th

Gratitude.

That's the word of the day. Brought to you by my counselor who suggested that I try to focus on the positive in my life to keep from feeling overwhelmed by the negative. So here I am and here I will be everyday for some time.

I got some catching up to do so I guess I can afford to reflect on what I should've been grateful for in the past:

I'm grateful for my alarm. Lord knows I'd never wake up & be on time for anything without it.

I'm grateful for my job. I'm grateful that I'm able to put food on my table and when this is over I'll be grateful to do more with my money than spend it on food.

I'm grateful for every restaurant within 25 mines that finally made it possible to order through a food delivery service. Definitely a top tier decision.

I'm more grateful for Netflix. Honestly I wouldn't know how else I'd be spending my time during Quarantine without it.

I'm exceedingly grateful that my girlfriend and friends never left my side. Even though I deserved it for how I shut down and essentially shut them out of my life.

Above all else, I'm just grateful that I still wake up everyday. Today is the first time in a long time that I can firmly say that.

Marathon

I remember my first practice.
I ran then I ran out of energy-
began walking and before long
wasn't sure if I had the ability
to run like the Usains and insane
long and mid-distance runners that
inspired me through the tv.

I remember my first marathon.
I ran.
3.1 miles I ran.
I ran.
6.2 miles I ran.
I ran.
13.1 miles I ran.
I ran.
25.2 miles I ran then I ran out of energy.
Began talking to myself
and instantly I knew
I had the ability
to run like the Bekeles
and let my legs
stride and glide me
exactly how I needed them;

to and through the last mile;
to and through my first, first place finish.

I went from walking to winning
In the same way you should go
from life to living.
Taking every day

Step by step.

Journal Entry: August 2nd

I thought to take a break from smoking trees
and walk amongst them instead;
One of my best decisions this year
if I say so myself.
So after walking a few trails I decided
to sit at a bench and just take
in the beauty that surrounded me.
I was overcome as feelings
flooded my mind and I struggled
to find words that could describe what I saw.

It's not perfect but here's what
I came up with after a few revisions:

A Brighter Blue

The leaves became Pom Poms
shaking rapidly & powerfully
as the breeze bristled through the trees.

The earth became a springboard
bouncing repeatedly with frenetic glee
caused by the jubilant, burrowing bugs
and insects that dwell beneath.

The sun became a blanket
warping graciously & covering
my body intimately with the same
warmth that nighttime meditation brings.

And the sky became
like something else entirely too,
Despite being embedded
in its numerous clouds,
It had certainly become
a brighter shade of blue.

Today is a beautiful day.

Public Confession: What I Have To Say

From my hairs on my head
To the soul laying dormant at my feet,
There's a sensation present;
presenting itself more and more menacing.

It keeps me up at night
Never truly able to be asleep,
It holds me down inside;
inside is a perpetual state of grief.

I fear that death is around the corner
chasing me in the way of my mortality.
With each day it's encroaching closer:
Closer for months I've felt it's presence
escalating from threat to impending inevitability.

Journal Entry: Documenting a Summer of Protests

I've been thinking about sharing my stories constructively about the recent outrage over social justice initiatives. I told Ms.Shaw about what happened earlier this year and how it all started and everything. She convinced me to try to write how I felt down. And I guess here we are. I haven't finished much but here's two things I've written kinda sorta on the subject.

Uncle Sam

Uncle Sam you brought me here:
Why does it seem like you wanna take me out?
First, you made me do tons of yard work-
I was young and it was too much to bear.
Seeing that you never took the time to help
I mean I know you fought yourself.
But it was just for that,
Yourself.
And this isn't a side note
even though you treat it like one.
But I'm gonna move on and past it
just like you always wanted me to.

I grew a little bit older and
as I did, production on the old house
we used to live in grew colder,
And so it seems with the hearts of men.
I know you saw me get bullied
but you never took the time to help.
You knew I was scared of trees and robes
regardless you were never there
to protect me from the ghosts.
I used to march, it's a pity that
you never took a stand with me…
or kneel and much less a seat.
People used to beat me like
when I was younger and everyday
I cried out to my mother.
You made up that we would be
together and equal but
I don't think you meant it yourself,
You couldn't've meant it yourself.
I guess I'm liable to steal in every store
I walk in because every worker
watches me from the moment I walk in.
The other day someone told me
I wanted something for free
as if to say I know your kind
and they were familiar with me.
And it amuses me that If

I ever steal I will get convicted
But my cousin can kill
and get his charges lifted-
Both of them actually;
The law enforcer and the one my age-
You know the one just like me
distinguishable by only our shade that is.
You said you would treat us
all the same regardless;
Can I ask what happened to that?
You're like a distant uncle to me
and a loving, embracing father to them.
I've done nothing wrong and
I've been wronged my entire life
but one more question because
I need to know the answer.
Uncle Sam,
It's clear that you love them.
What have I ever done to make you
not love me?

Carson Oliver Patrick-Simpleton

What do you see when you look at me?
Is there a fire brewing in my eyes
as red as the stripes you hold onto
so dearly when you claim that
you have not profiled me?

What are you listening for when you hear me?
Do you care about what I'm saying-
or does the meter make you forget that
it's running until you feel that the price
of my bars can't be paid
with dollar bills but my life instead?

What do you feel when you play
with my hair follicles?
Does it feel like wool, cotton, sheep-
or something else more animalistic
than humane because I've noticed you like
to pet it as if it were while you slam
my head in the concrete.

What do you smell when you breathe me in?
Do I reek of gunpowder and 2 for the 15?
Well sorry if I do;

I never washed the scent of my tears away when
the cops gunned downed
a couple young men from my crew
that I grew up with.

What do you taste when
my name is across your tongue?
Am I overly salty or-
bitter over my experiences or-
am I well seasoned to your
hateful and envious ways?

I wonder what I am to you everyday when I see
you roaming the streets in my neighborhood.
I wonder what you see when you look into the
eyes of my brothers because you become so
fearful;
I've never seen in them whatever you do
on a regular basis around here.

I wonder what I am to you everyday when
I'm playing baseball at the rec. center and
I see you parked out on the sidewalk
and why sometimes you mistake
the crack of the bat for a gunshot;
we're only stealing bases but you seem
tense as if we were stealing diamonds.

I wonder what I am to you everyday
when you have a 'feeling' that
something is going to happen.
Did you also have a feeling that Shareef
had a gun or did you feel or
pat him down to figure it out?

I can't figure out what I am to you when you
claim that you smell something in the air.
Do you sense something so toxic in the air
that you have to strangle all the oxygen
out of me to better ensure my safety?

I can't figure out what I am to you when
you harass me hoping you can
catch me doing something I shouldn't.
I feel like I'm just a steak that you feast on
to make sure that your children are fed at night.

You're always looking to put my brothers
and I in a to-go box and preserve me until
you've expired all my other options
in life so I have to-go back
into the confines of another cold box.

To you I might as well be a barren

silhouette or a shadow in the alleyway;
a shady individual.
Because you refuse to recognize me
for what I am,
You only recognize the color of my skin
as if it resembles who I am-
Past
Present
and future if graciously gifted to me.
I ask what I am to you
and though you've never said it,
I know clearly what your answer is.

Just because I'm black doesn't mean
that I am a villainous character
you have to pay special attention to.
Just because I'm black doesn't mean
that I'm a dirty immoral individual
whose soul needs cleansing.
And one day you'll realize that
I shouldn't be treated differently
because my skin looks different.

Journal Entry: November Reign

November is always a crazy month. I rediscovered some old notes and scrap papers I had written in previous years while cleaning out my desk. They reminded me of the incredible highs and excruciating lows that characterize this month from year to year. I'd thought it'd be good to record them here as well as my current thoughts and feelings as I write today. Kinda like a change and continuity over my lifetime kinda thing. Even FaceTimed with my friends about our current state of affairs and shared my thoughts as well. Here's what came out of it all:

November 2008

Last November doubt was blowing
in my face like hurricane winds,

I was about to test out the polls because school
wasn't working like unemployment.

I was about to grab my lighter because my job
wasn't providing enough to keep the lights on.

I was selling candy bars on the side for profit but
the voice encouraging me to switch over to bags
was starting to sound a lot like God.

But then last November I saw my president and
his brown face looked just like mine.
His figure was just like mine.
His story was just like mine.

He said "Yes We Can"
and I believed that I could too.

I can get above the poverty line
without having to give out lines
on the side while I'm taking orders at work,
I can achieve goals and kick

for myself instead of receiving punts,
I can calmly face doubt during a storm
and know that I'll be fine because I'm in the eye:
and I can see future goals
turn into my past achievements.

In November 2008 he said "Yes We Can,"
and he served as the proof that made me believe
that statement was true.

November 2016

It was raining.
People were crying-
or were the tears
the rain that reigned
from the clouds up above?
I'm not sure to tell the truth
and it would be an
alternative fact to say otherwise.

But it was raining
and there were people
crying in the streets
searching for justice
and lying upside down
on their beds puzzling
How and when something
like this could happen.

Last November,
Doubt wasn't just blowing
in my face like hurricane winds-
It came in and took roofs off the
houses of the living.

I tested out the polls for the

first time only to find that in the end,
People would be stripped
of their voting rights
and that sickened me
the more it sank in.

I thought I was going
to be able to grab my lighter
and wave my hands higher
but I know I will have to take a San Francisco
trademarked knee before I can afford to take a
seat.

I believed my candy bar
business could turn big profits but
It seems like I'll only be left with Marks;
No Jacobs. No Daniels. & No Ishmaels.

Last November I saw
my president and his brown face-
that looked just like mine
leave office and try to convince
me that everything would be fine.
His figure said otherwise.
The story may prove otherwise.

He yelled one more time "Yes We Can"

but I think it got lost under the loud speaker who
screamed "Make America Great Again".

In November 2008 he said those same words-
"Yes We Can,"
And I believed them.
It's now November 2016.
The climate is different.
and frankly I'm not as confident
in our ability to do it over again.

American President: A Comparative Essay Sparked By A FaceTime Conversation About the Last Eight Years

You gave the other your dollars,
he gave you back more of the same.
When you gave the new one dollars,
he gave you back change.

Change that resulted in more jobs
and less unemployment.
Change that halted the price of oil and expanded
an economy that had been stagnant.
Change that happened to make love legal,
church and state separate.

Y'all wanted a stricter foreign policy-
well Obama took down a known
bomber during his presidency.

Y'all wanted housing and a better market
Which his department delivered among other
things but yet and still y'all considered electing
John McCain who's from the same party
that collapsed the whole damn thing!

Some of y'all wanted to live but couldn't
until he signed a bill that wouldn't

allow for anyone to go without health insurance-
insuring us that no one would have to die simply
because of their poor socio-economic status.

He kept some of y'all on this earth
but that didn't stop some of y'all from
running his name through the dirt.
You rejected and disrespected him
as a person and tried to discredit him
despite how good he had been to
Every. Last. American.

Not one scandal while he was in office.
A feat that no one else can boast
who has ever held office
and somehow, someway he became
the official scapegoat-
He was a donkey but he was treated like a jackass
and blamed for the legislation that wouldn't pass
through congress as if congress was his address.
The White House wasn't getting foreclosed-
It wasn't his fault why Republicans and
Democrats couldn't find a way to make way
for the overdue bills that piled up.
It's not his fault they couldn't get a resolution-
I know he resolved his responsibilities
but he can't resolve what's supposed

to be done by house and senate committees
So take your anger and send it
to the right address please.

In an era of big business
He made it his business to raise minimum wage
and make sure that everyone got paid.
I mean how could you not like that?
How could you argue against that-
and what type of person would
try to fight back against that-
that type of progress?

I guess no matter how far we
move in the right direction
Some people just won't be satisfied unless
it's the right that's doing the progressing-
I guess that's why they elected Trump
instead of Hilary in this past election.

Someone who can't fit the shoes-
or even the gloves
of Mr.44-
The President that cared
more about the real issues
and not more about the petty
twitter feuds.

Obama is an honest man
who lives an honest life
with his wife and two kids
but his predecessor lies
constantly and is known
for being ruthless and having
a lucrative business...
I won't forget about Trump University.
And the people who you scammed
will have the same kind of memory.

We all know that most times the sequel
sucks but I can't even call this a sequel
because Obama believed everyone was
equal but Trump wants to build a wall
and kick out all the so-called "Illegal People".

In fact-
He still has yet to utter one.
But in factual
he still doesn't even have an actual
stance on issues-
He just flip flops and to this point has been all
sandals as if he's on vacation and doesn't take
this vacation seriously.
Seriously, he might as well be gray

because Obama made his mission clear as black
and white and Trump is as shady as a Walter
White alibi.

So I ask-
who is the real American President?

The one that won the popular vote or
the one who boasted about his one percentage
status the most?

Is it the one who unified citizens
or is it the one that promises to get rid
and alienate some of them?

Is it the one who was wrongfully called a Muslim
or the one that is wrongfully calling out muslims?

Is it the one who made America great again
after a near depression
or the one who's just saying he'll make
 America great again and causing
a different type of depression?

Is it the one who took precautions
to stop & contain the public health concern
Ebola,

or is it the one that continued to lie,
spread misinformation & downplay Corona?

Because the way you treated the former,
and have begged respect for the latter
Has started to make me question
what it means to be America's President.

Understand

Understand that I never wanted
to be your shoulder to lean on.
Your tears hit my neck and flow south
till the stories you speak turn into a creek
in the bloodstream of my capillaries;
Hard felt, they, in my heart they are felt.

Understand that I don't want
to be a shoulder for you to lean on.
I grow weaker and weaker and weaker still-
Still trying to figure out how to hold you up
When I can't stand on my feet my damn self.

Understand that it tears my soul apart
to be your shoulder to lean on.
Physically.
Mentally.
Spiritually.
I'm e x h a u s t e d.

I will not do it no more.

I   Have   Had   Enough.

I am in the dressing room putting on my armor.

I am outside the café sending warnings from across the street.

I am in broad daylight strapped and I don't give a fuck about concealed carry.

I am taking matters into my own hands-
On behalf of Lady Justice and all the black women that haven't been dealt justice-
I've had enough.

Understand that I never wanted
to be your shoulder to lean on:
When you weren't allowed to be yourself-
When you were taken and remained unfound-
When you were under treated by doctors-
When you were mistreated by men-
When you were the antecedent of a movement
you started just to be carted off
your own platform
the moment attention is shown.

Understand that I never again will fulfill the role
of your shoulder to lean on once we've
dealt with the issues that have strained you.

I heard your voice.
I witnessed what they did from afar.
I felt your pain.
And now I will act and call upon everyone
I know to act until you don't need
my shoulder anymore.

Watching Short Films: This One Is About Friends

I still watch short films.

Watched at least one hundred
or so on Omeleto alone.

I've watched tons of them
but one of them still sticks with me.
In this one short film of theirs
this kid kills his best friend in an accident.

I rewatched this short film, and I related to it too.

Thought about Shareef at least a few times
and how hard his loss hit home.

I sat with it for a while.
I was watching the news the other day
and this anchor blamed his family & friends
for not telling him he can't wear a hoodie in
public.

I watch short films, but I don't live through them.

There's a million things
I am completely responsible for.
But as much as I've felt guilty
I know that his passing wasn't my fault.

Libations

Tonight we're gonna do something different.
I want all in attendance (in other words just me)
to join in and help me commemorate this past
year.

Now raise a glass for every
anti-mask patriot that fought
tirelessly for our freedoms.

Pour one out for those dedicated
civilians that died in the line of duty
roaming public spaces to protect
our first amendment rights.

Follow that up by taking a shot for the 600K
and counting that didn't make it to see this day.

Raise another glass
for our beloved armchair doctors.

Were they experts, no.
Were they well read, no.
Did they at least study the science???
No but they gave unnecessary advice

so pour one out for them too.
Take a shot for those
that listened to their "expert" advice as well,
they needed at least one but decided that
Pfizer wasn't good enough.

Raise a glass for
the cops that abuse their power.

Don't pour one out this time though.
Violence always pours out
onto the street once they're
done fucking up anyway.

And save this shot too.
Too many shots have already been fired.

For those us you still playing
take a double shot in solidarity
for the victims of Asian hate crimes.
Take another double if you've had
a couple loved ones snatched from your life.
Pour one more good one out-
No not the liquor, this time shed a tear-
Pour out over the pain you've felt this past year.

2.21.21

I drank to your remembrance.

My body, my temple.
A sweet liqueur seized the entrance;
Entranced I felt the rush again.
The rush, the joyful glee of having people like family and family friends next to me.

I drank to your remembrance.

My body, my temple.
A bittersweet harmony caressed all in attendance;
Enriched I felt a pulse again.
The high, the unparalleled peace of having people like family and family friends next to me.

I drank to your remembrance.

My body, my temple.
A victorious scream echoed throughout the fortress and out through the exit.
Enticed I felt the spirit again.

The spirit, the souls I would disappoint in the afterlife if I were to give in to vice.

I drank to your remembrance
and I got drunk to my own detriment.
But I've already learned that lesson
and I won't allow myself to fall back
into a state of regression.

Discontinued

Tens of millions of years ago a meteor pummeled the earth wiping out the dinosaurs and an estimated 75% of all living species went extinct.

Discontinued.

A few thousand years ago an ice age swooped over the earth's surface & since great predators like saber tooth cats and great prey like mammoths have fallen alike.

Discontinued.

A few hundred years ago a plague ushered itself across Eurasia & North Africa resulting in an unprecedented number of human casualties.

Discontinued.

So tens of millions of years ago a meteor hit the earth and killed dinosaurs yet small mammals were able to survive and thrive.

Continue.

So a few thousand years ago an ice age came and proved to be too cold for even wool coated mammoths and furry tigers yet humans survived.

Continue.

So a few hundred years ago a plague came and went with no medical solutions available and yet humanity survived.

Continue.

As we speak we find ourselves in another pandemic but I know we will-

Continue.

At this moment black people, asian people, women & queer people still face oppression but it won't always-

Continue.

Right now I'm mourning the loss of a friend and family member but I know my healing will-

Continue.

Despite all the immense pain, suffering & unforeseen tragedy we will come to experience life will always continue on.

Discontinued.

Thiscontinued.

This Continues

Appendix: Notes & Acknowledgements

Headlines
    Reference: In the early 20th century Tulsa Oklahoma was one of the most prominent concentrations of African-American businesses in the United States. The city was commonly referred to as America's "Black Wall Street". The city was burned by white residents in what would later be referred to as the Tulsa race massacre of 1921.

Gilligan's Island
    Reference: The name is a reference to the popular 1960s tv show of the same name.

New Hobby: Watching Short Films
    Reference: Omeleto is a real Youtube channel devoted to sharing short films to a larger audience.

Flying Spirit
    Reference: Soft allusion to both the Spirit Airlines Brand and the popular phrase "fighting spirit".

Black Ties
Reference: The heading is a play on words with three separate and distinct meanings for each of the individual poems that share the heading. Despite their distinct meanings, together they form a shared greater perspective on the cultural reality of the black experience in America through time and popular tradition.

A History of Black Ties
Reference: The United States has a long history of race related violence and hate crimes. Most reports suggest that at least 4,000 African Americans were lynched in the 19th and 20th century. The Bur Oak Tree was accounted for a number of lynchings in Tulsa Oklahoma. The 19th and 20th century years provided in the poem correlate to actual historical lynchings whereas the last year (2020) symbolizes how organized violence against black people still persists to this day. It persists in many social institutions and maybe most prominently within policing. In other ways, violence has evolved from overt assailants to covert prejudice.

An Occasion of Black Ties

Reference: Barbecues, cookouts and religious gatherings have all played a role in a mainstream cultural heritage for Black Americans. These gatherings have been a way for the black community to bond, unite, and come together even in spite of the day to day hardships.

A Black Tie Affair

Reference: Funerals are emotionally resonant, strange and melancholic affairs. This is in part due to the fact that the relationship you have to another person does not end when they pass away. They are in a way both gone and still with you at the same time.

The Island of Misfit Toys

Reference: The title is a reference to the popular movie "Rudolph the Red-Nosed Reindeer and the Island of Misfit Toys" (2001).

The Start of An All Encompassing Journal

Reference: Dr.Kimberly Shaw is a fictional character from the show Melrose Place.

Crisis Actor
Reference: Henry Cavill is the current Superman in the DC Universe. Jeffrey Hudson was a jester for English queen Henrietta Maria of France in the 17th century.

Just Be A Building
Reference: "the few, the proud the marines" US Navy slogan. "What's Your Warrior?" US army slogan.

Uncle Sam
Reference: Common national personification of the United States.

Carson Oliver Patrick-Simpleton
Reference: Personification of the national police force of the United States.

Libations
Reference: A libation is a ritual pouring of a liquid in memory of the dead.

Special Acknowledgments

I would like to thank my family and close friends for all the support they have provided me to this day. Without them I wouldn't be the person who I am now doing what I do and I will forever be thankful for everyone who plays a crucial role in my life. Thank you guys for all the support!

Special thanks to my loyal team of editors and friends who have spent countless hours reading, reviewing, and providing constructive criticism of my work.

Special thanks to my amazing friend and awesome photographer and film director Aaron who graced me with headshots again! Follow him on IG @awilsonw and check out some more of his work on his site awilsonw.com.

Finally, I would like to thank every last one of you who bought this book. I appreciate the support and please leave a review and share with a friend.

LeShane is a black poet, spoken word artist, and writer from New Jersey. He first began gaining notoriety as a writer after the success of "Open Mic Night: Campus Programs That Champion College Student Voice and Engagement". He was awarded an "Outstanding Book Award" from the AERA for my contributions to the collaborative book. In 2018, he published his first of two acclaimed chapbooks "Is It Wonderful,". That same year he released his second chapbook "Sunflower BLVD". In 2020, he released his first full length anthology "Our Chemically Altered Romance," to critical acclaim.

Milton Keynes UK
Ingram Content Group UK Ltd.
UKHW021340251024
2386UKWH00060B/914